Lemington & Newburn Then and Now

by George Nairn &
West Newcastle Picture History Collection

The Point, Lemington. 3736

Industrial buildings at Lemington on what was known as 'The Point' or Canary Island around 1920s. The Bridge on the left over 'The Gut' was near the site of the old coal staithes.

Previous page: A postcard of 'Newburn on Tyne'. A view from St Michael and All Angels Church.

Summerhill Books

Summerhill Books publishes local history books on Northumberland, Durham and Tyneside. To receive a catalogue of our titles send a stamped addressed envelope to:

Summerhill Books, PO Box 1210, Newcastle-upon-Tyne NE99 4AH

or email: summerhillbooks@yahoo.co.uk

or visit our website to view our full range of books: **www.summerhillbooks.co.uk**

Postage and packaging is FREE on all UK orders.

Copyright George Nairn & West Newcastle Picture History Collection

First published in 2011 by

Summerhill Books
PO Box 1210, Newcastle-upon-Tyne NE99 4AH

ISBN: 978-1-906721-44-2

Contents

Introduction

Lemington and Newburn have a long and interesting history and this book is a celebration of the two communities' heritage and their people. The starting point is a series of 'then and now' photographs of the area. Comparing old images with modern views is becoming a popular way of exploring local history. Many of the 'then' photographs in the book have come from George Nairn who is a postcard collector and author of numerous publications on the North East. The remaining illustrations have been supplied by the West Newcastle Picture History Collection who have been archiving old photographs of the area since 1984.

It was often a hard task to find all of the 'now' photographs. Finding the original locations was sometimes difficult or the view today was obscured by trees that had grown substantially over the past hundred years. The photographer of the old pictures also had the advantage of been able to stand in the middle of the road if we wished. These were the days when traffic was not as busy as it is now. Avoiding been knocked down was only one of the obstacles faced by today's photographer. However, the majority of the 'now' images are very good comparisons and give the reader an idea of how much has changed over the past century. They also, occasionally, show how little has changed.

As well as 'then and now' photographs there are many more old pictures of how life once was in Lemington and Newburn. Work is featured, including: Spencer's Steel Works; the Glass Works; the railways; and transport. Everyday life is shown with people at school, in church or out shopping as well as social activities such as the cinema, pubs and sport. Finally, there are old pictures of 'Days to Remember' that show local people at special events or representing their community or simply enjoying themselves.

Andrew Clark
Summerhill Books, 2011

'Greetings from Newburn & District' – A multiview postcard from around 1950. The five views show: Post Office Corner (top left); Hexham Road, Throckley (top right); Engine Inn, Walbottle (bottom left); Wesleyan Church and Council Offices (bottom right); and the Parish Church (centre).

History in Postcards

This view is from a coloured postcard titled 'Post Office, Tyne View, Lemington'. The card was sent to 34 Tulloch Street, Scotswood Road on 31st July 1905. The message on the back reads: 'Hope you will like this one for your collection.' The collecting of postcards is still a hobby for many. The Golden Age of the postcard was from 1900 until the 1920s.

POST OFFICE, TYNE VIEW, LEMINGTON.

Two postmarks of Newburn and Lemington from the backs of postcards included in this book. Today we rarely send a postcard; perhaps only from a holiday destination. One hundred years ago sending a postcard was as common as an email or text message now. Some of the messages on the back of postcards from a century ago are as simple as 'How are you?' or 'Will see you soon' – the sort of things we say electronically now. On the backs of some postcards are

messages such as 'See you this afternoon.' You could post a card first thing in the morning and it would arrive at its destination by the second post later that day. With digital cameras you can post a photograph on Facebook or send images from your phone to share with friends and family. A postcard was sent to people you knew in the same way. On page nine is a postcard with the message on the back saying: 'This is a view of the next village.'

Millfield Crescent, Newburn around 1920s. This is a postcard produced by Gateshead photographer Robert Johnston. His postcards were called the Monarch Series and can be recognised by the style of captions in the left hand corner and their unique numbers. He produced thousands of postcards throughout the North East. This postcard has the number '4950'. On

Millfield Crescent, Newburn. 4950

page 26 there is a Johnston postcard of 'Newburn Lane and Police Station'. That has the number '4953' and means the two photographs were taken on the same day.

Looking Back at Lemington

In 1937 the booklet 'Our Parish' was published to celebrate the centenary of the consecration of the Holy Saviour Church, Sugley. Written by Mabel Waldram and assisted by George Cockburn, the booklet gave this account of the early days of Lemington:

'Slowly the morning mists rolled up from the river, revealing the green hills and fertile plains of Lemington. The Lark soared high above her nest. Her song was accompanied by raucous voices of the keel-men, singing, whistling (for they were a jolly crowd) and shouting orders as they piled their wherries between the different jetties.

'The river in this year of grace – 1836 – presented a busy scene. It was dotted with craft of strange and crude design, which bartered for and carried goods up and down the busy waterway, sometimes even venturing across the sea. It was a goodly sight that met the eye of the keelman, as he gazed towards the Vale of Sugley.

'Low Lemington, with its neat row of tiny cottages set at various angles, little odd cottages, which seemed to have escaped from the rows and settled down alone and aloof in their wide bright gardens – the busy staithes, built in 1638.

'The green, which rolled happily down to the water's edge; and behind all these casting a shadow of great importance, brooded the three mighty cones of Lemington Glassworks. Built in 1787 each cone was 70 feet high with walls 4 feet thick. With sphinx-like solemnity they meditated upon the changing fortunes of the river, even gazing unflinchingly upon the new altogether marvellous wagonway, running from Wylam to Lemington Staithes. Silhouetted against the sky, they were a landmark for miles and the germ of the small community that surrounded them ...

An illustration of the Old Tyne Iron Works in 1835.

'Through the trees, away to the west, one could discern the noble gables of Lemington Hall, built in 1787, by a French nobleman who fled from his country during the revolution.

'To the right as the eye travelled up the Bywell Bank, were the Ironworks – erected in 1797. Here an enterprising trade of smelting and manufacture of iron was carried on, the coal coming from Wylam by means of an inclined plane formed of cast iron. The works were discontinued in 1875.

'A little higher up and further to the right – amid gardens, orchards and trees – were the picturesque houses of Sugley Field, the residence of Chas. Balmer, manager of the Ironworks, on the edge of Dene.

'The wide, deep village pond, with its families of water-fowl, its reed and weeping willows, skirted the bottom of the gardens. This was the rendezvous of merry skaters on the winter evenings. Tradition had it that the pond was an old pit-working which had subsided and become flooded.'

'Our Parish' is a fascinating history of Sugley and Lemington from 1836 to 1937. It features the development of the churches, schools, shops, pubs, industry and the social life of the area.

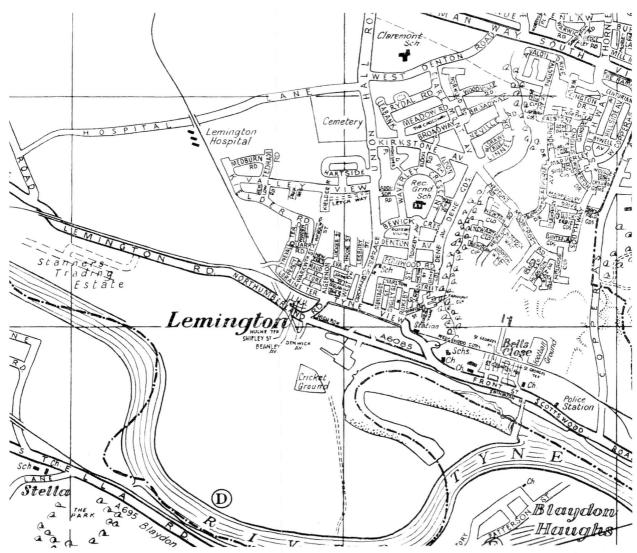

A map of Lemington from the 1950s. Since this map was drawn there has been further housing development in the area – particularly around Hospital Lane.

Lemington Secondary School before the Second World War. It became Lemington Grammar School after 1945. Hundreds of local children went to this school in what are called 'the best days of your life'.

Here are three photographs of the old community of Sugley.

Right: Children from Sugley School in 1887. At that time there were around 190 attending the school. On the left is Mr Prudhoe (assistant) and on the right is Mr Sladin (headmaster). The pupils include: F. Leybourn, E. and I. Hutton, Cameron Forster, J. Turnbull, W.I. Thompson, J. Readhead, J.R. Routledge, J. and T. Wilkinson and J., T., A, and R. Jacques.

Left: The west end of Sugley Field Cottages that were pulled down in 1906. In the centre of the photograph was Granny Atkinson's Black Bullet shop. Little is known of Granny Atkinson except if she was selling 'black bullets' she obviously ran a sweet shop.

Right: Sugley Village Pond around 1906.

The 1937 booklet 'Our Parish' describes what happened to Sugley Pond and Cottages:

'In 1906, Sugley Field Cottages were demolished, and the pond, with its fringe of trees and verge of grass, drained. Thus was destroyed the

pleasant picture of sylvan beauty which greeted the traveller as he crossed the railway bridge. The ruthless hand of progress could not be stayed; a wave of prosperity was sweeping the district. Lemington was developing steadily. The growth of John Spencer's Steel Works meant the growth of the surrounding area. Streets began to encroach upon green fields in every direction.'

A view of Low Lemington with the Glass Works to the right. This was a postcard sent from Newburn to Middlesbrough in 1916. The message reads: 'This is a view of the next village.' There appears to be other industry along this part of the Tyne with small factories and jetties by the riverbank.

A multiview postcard of Lemington from around 1910. The Glass Works is in the centre with Tyne View (top left); Loraine Terrace (top right); Panniers (bottom right); Bridge over the Dene (bottom left). The postcard is a mixture of urban, rural and industrial and the area retained those three themes for many years.

Low Row, Lemington at the end of nineteenth century. These properties were very near the Glass Works and the building on the right was probably part of the works. Out in the street are poss tubs and mangles – so this is likely to be Monday (Wash day). Most housewives had their weekly agenda and had a job for each day. Monday was the day for washing clothes etc; Tuesday was for ironing; Wednesday might be cleaning inside the house; Thursday was for baking; Friday would be cleaning outside of the house with the swilling of yards and donkey stoning of steps; Saturday was for shopping – if there was money; finally Sunday was for church.

Low Row, Lemington around 1890 with white-washed cottages on the left.

Tynevale Terrace, around 1920. On the right is J. Curry's butchers. A young girl looks in the window for good cuts of meat.

Tynevale Terrace in 2011. J. Curry's butchers is now gone and like many corner shops has been converted into a house. Most of the houses have lost the iron railings they had in the 1920s. The railings were probably collected during the Second World War when there was a campaign to collect as much metal as possible.

Tyne View showing a tram passing the Co-op around 1920. On the left is the post office opened in 1886. A boy is pulling a handcart and it looks like he is getting some help from the man beside him.

Lemington News and Post Office, Tyne View in 2011. This photograph was taken further up Tyne View than the one above. The old post office is in the middle of the picture and is unused at the moment – although there is a cash point machine in the wall. The Co-op Building has gone and now The Lemington Centre stands on the site.

Tyne View at the junction with Orchard Terrace, around 1900. Behind the two girls is the Lemington Branch of Lloyds Bank. Facing the bank is the Station Hotel (right of the photograph). The name above the door is William Scott.

Tyne View and Orchard Terrace in 2011. Lloyds Bank has been replaced by Wilson Defraine Property Services. The Station Hotel was demolished in the 1990s.

Loraine Terrace, around 1905. In the distance, on the corner of Percy Street, are some shops. At one time most streets had a shop at the corner and communities such as Lemington had a wide variety of local businesses. Today many of these shops are long gone as we buy more goods from supermarkets or the internet.

Loraine Terrace in 2011. The shops on Percy Street are now closed, however the surface of the road is in a much better condition.

Eva Street in 1905. On the left is the sign for George Murray's grocers on the corner of Lesbury Street.

Eva Street in 2011. This photograph was taken at the end of the street. Like most streets today, there are a number of cars parked outside people's homes. A hundred years ago it would be rare to see a car in Lemington. At that time the speed limit on all roads was 20 mph and there were no driving tests!

Algernon Road, around 1905. On the right is the High Club. Behind the club is Maud Street. R.E. Laybourn had a shop at the corner of Algernon Road and Maud Street. An advert from the 1930s said: 'For Quality, Cleanliness and Civility … Noted for Fried Fish.' The Methodist Church is at the end of the road on the right.

Algernon Road in 2011. The High Club is still popular as is the Methodist Church. A new building has replaced the houses on the left and one side of Maud Street (just past the club) has been demolished. Behind Maud Street is Store Street that was once used as a location for filming a Catherine Cookson television drama.

Algernon Road, around 1905. On the right is Robson's shop – family grocer and confectioner – with a fine display of goods in the window. There is a large group of children outside the houses posing for the photograph. This postcard would probably have been sold in the shop. How many local families bought this card and kept it as a treasured family photograph?

Algernon Road in 2011. The shop on the right is the only building to survive a century later. The shop is now a Londis and its window display is very different from the one above. Now, local shops rarely have displays to attract their customers.

Looking Back at Newburn

Kelly's Directory of Durham & Northumberland of 1902 has this description of Newburn:

'Newburn is a parish and village on the northern bank of the River Tyne, here crossed by an iron bridge, erected in 1894, and affording access from the village to the railway station at Ryton, on the Newcastle and Carlisle section of the North Eastern Railway; this place also has a station on the Scotswood, Newburn and Wylam branch of the same system (opened July, 1885); and is five miles west from Newcastle-upon-Tyne …

'In the village are the extensive works of John Spencer and Sons Limited, for the manufacture of steel castings, forgings, plates for boilers and ships, tools, steel files and springs of all kinds.

'There are salmon fisheries at Newburn and Lemington Point belonging to the Duke of Northumberland.

'On 28th August, 1640, at the opening of the Second Campaign of Charles I against the Scots, Edward Viscount Conway and General Leslie, leaving two-thirds of their forces in Newcastle, posted themselves with 3,000 foot and 1,500 horses at the ford at Newburn, 4 miles above the town, and there threw up hasty entrenchments; these however, were commanded by the higher ground on the opposite bank of the river, and as the Scots also mounted their cannon (rude

A postcard of the Parish Church.

engines made of bar iron and hooped with cord and wet raw hides) on the church tower, the undisciplined force of the Royalist commanders wavered, and being thereupon attacked by the Scots, whom they had permitted to cross the river; were completely defeated and dispersed; and on the day following the Scots occupied Newcastle.'

There is a monument commemorating the Battle of Newburn Ford in the Newburn County Park.

An illustration of 'Old Newburn'.

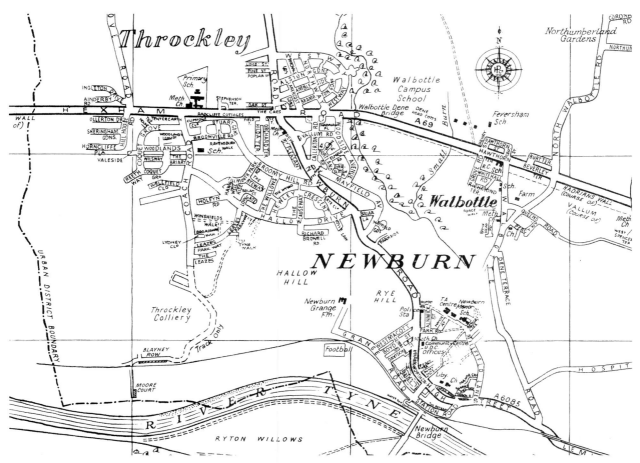

A map of Newburn from the 1950s. On the left is the boundary of Newburn Urban District. At the bottom of the map is marked Ryton Willows – a popular destination for day-trippers from throughout the region for many years.

A drawing of Newburn from the south bank of the Tyne from around 1888. This is a very rural scene, although by this time, the end of the nineteenth century, Newburn was becoming more industrialised.

Newburn showing Institute. 4946

An unusual view of Newburn showing the Institute from around 1920s. The photographer appears to have taken this picture from the railway line. Station Road is in the foreground and by the road are long, well-kept gardens. This photograph and the one below are by Gateshead photographer Robert Johnston.

The Bridge, Newburn. 3898

A postcard titled 'The Bridge, Newburn' from around 1920s. The card was sent to Morpeth and the message on the back reads: 'I arrived home safely but now wished I had stopped as mother is spring cleaning and I am beating carpets and cleaning windows.' To the far right are the chimneys of the Steel Works. By the banks of the river a steam engine and some wagons can just be seen. The old railway line is now a public footpath.

The High Street, looking west, around 1900. In the centre of the picture are the twelve Almshouses, built in 1870 at a cost of around £3,000, that still stand today. At the time of this photograph the rents were 7 shillings and sixpence for single people and 10 shillings and sixpence for a married couple. The road beyond the cart looks quite narrow and in later years the High Street was widened to allow more traffic.

Newburn High Street, looking east, in the early 1900s. On the left is a shop – a rare sight in High Street at that time. Kelly's trade directory of 1902 lists only one High Street shop and that was Daniel Snowdon, grocer. The shop and the buildings around it are now gone and have been replaced by flats.

Newburn Then & Now

Newburn Lane & Police Station, Newburn. 4953

A Johnston postcard of 'Newburn Lane and Police Station' from around 1920s. The Police Station, built in 1911, is at the far end of the road on the right. In the distance is a tram and in front of it is a steam traction engine. On the right is the Presbyterian Church that was later used by an antiques dealer.

Newburn Road in 2011. The tram and traction engine have now been replaced with cars. The building on the right is now the Kingdom Hall of the Jehovah Witnesses.

POLICE STATION & NEWBURN LANE.

A postcard of the 'Police Station and Newburn Lane'. The message on the back reads: 'This is a view of our Police Station, as I promised you will see it is a fine big place. Hoping this finds you all well, as it leaves me very canny.' This postcard was published by T. Smith of Grange Road, Newburn.

Newburn Road in 2011. The Police Station is now apartments and its iron railings replaced by a wall. The rest of the road has not changed too much over the past 100 years.

Station Road, around 1920s. The Newburn Hotel is on the left. Further up the road a lorry is unloading goods outside one of the shops. In the early 1900s there were the following shops on Station Road: Miss Esther Bishop (confectioner); Joseph Davison (butcher); Thomas Dawe (general store); and Thomas Nixon (grocer).

Station Road in 2011. Sadly the Newburn Hotel is no longer open but the road still has local shops. Newburn & District War Memorial stands at the top of the road beyond the traffic lights.

A postcard titled 'Post Office, Newburn-on-Tyne' that was sent to Wylam in 1903. At this time Thomas Nixon was the sub-postmaster. Letters would arrive at 7.10 am, 3.05 pm & 6.05 pm. Letters were dispatched at 9 am & 11.15 am and 6 pm & 8 pm; 7.45 pm on Sundays. This was a very good service, however, in those days letters were the main form of communication for the majority of people. Today this is a very busy junction but 100 years ago only a horse and cart are in the road.

The Post Office in 2011. Now they offer services such as motor vehicle licences, travel and banking. Letters and parcels are still posted from here – but fewer today than in the past when we now have telephones and emails as alternatives. Next door to the Post Office is M. Thompson Pet Foods. Malcolm Thompson has run this shop since 1986.

Newburn Road with the Council Offices and Wesleyan Church. Newburn Urban District Council was formed in 1893 and ceased in 1974 when Tyne & Wear Council was created and the area became part of Newcastle. The Council Offices were opened in 1911 and at that time comprised the townships of Newburn, Newburn Hall, East Denton, West Denton, Sugley, Throckley and Walbottle.

Newburn Road in 2011. The Council Offices now stand empty after being used for some time as a housing office. The Wesleyan Chapel has been replaced by, appropriately, Chapel Court. The chapel was built in 1895 and closed in 1965. In the 1970s the building was used as a depot for a book supplier and then was demolished in 1996.

COUNCIL OFFICES & WESLEYAN CHURCH, NEWBURN.

02342

A closer view of the Council Offices and Wesleyan Church.

The former Council Offices and Chapel Court in 2011.

The High Street in 1900 with the impressive Newburn Working Men's Club and Institute on the far left. Two carts, going in opposite directions, have stopped in the middle of the road. This would cause traffic problems today. Are they having a chat about business or were they asked to 'act natural' by the photographer?

Newburn High Street in 2011. The Institute building was closed and became a residential home in the 1990s. The road alongside the old Institute has been widened with several buildings demolished. No carts in the road today but plenty of cars now drive along this normally busy road. The area on the right keeps a similar shape with a slight rise to housing set back.

A closer view of the 'Club'. This is from a coloured postcard sent from Newburn to Sunderland in 1904. At this time there were 1,600 members of the Institute. Kelly's Directory of Durham & Northumberland from 1902 says the Working Men's Club had a 'curator' called James Sim. On the right is a drinking fountain.

The old 'Club' in 2011 with the buildings on the right of the photograph above now gone. A conservatory has been added to the Institute building replacing the old entrance shown above.

A view of the High Street, looking east, in 1972. Towering above the villages at this time was the Percy Pit spoil heap where waste from nearby collieries had been dumped for many years. At its height it rose to over 60 feet above the Lemington to Newburn road. The heap was lowered in the 1980s and the spoil distributed around the area.

The High Street in 2011. The pit heap has gone and now its the trees that tower above the streets. They were only saplings in the photograph from 1972. The flats on the left have been modernised in recent years.

The Almshouses at Newburn from an Auty Series postcard. Auty of Tynemouth was one of the earliest postcard publishers and had started in the 1890s. There are other Auty postcards of Newburn on pages 22 and 37. A workman is busy to the left while some children are in the foreground. A few people stand by the doors of the houses – residents perhaps?

The Almshouses in 2011 – continuing to provide homes for local people.

A postcard of 'Old Village, Newburn' printed and published for T. Smith, Grange Road, Newburn. Talbot Smith was a local newsagent. It was sent to a farm in Carlisle in 1915.

The High Street in 2011. The old Head Offices of Spencer's Steel Works are on the right. Next door is a Dental Surgery – a private house in the photograph above. The house past the Surgery, before the Almshouses, is one of the oldest in the area. A sign on the house says: 'Erected by Hugh, Duke of Northumberland Lord of the Manor, 1822.'

STEEL WORKS AND OFFICES, NEWBURN.   "Auty Series." G.H., W.B. 2477.

An Auty Series postcard of the Steel Works and Offices from around 1900. A centenary brochure produced by the works in 1910 declared: 'The village of Newburn, as the result of the enterprise of John Spencer & Sons, Limited, has developed into a thriving and vigourous community whose interests are bound up with those of the Firms.'

The old Steel Works Offices in 2011. The offices are now empty and awaiting a new tenant. The rest of the scene above has completely changed and the works no longer dominate the skyline of Newburn.

The Steel Works

John Spencer & Sons Steel Works, Newburn around 1901. The firm moved from Newcastle to Newburn in 1822.

John Spencer, born 1785, the founder of the Steel Works. He died in Lemington Hall in 1867.

The Newburn Official Guide of the 1950s gave this account of the Steel Works:

'In the year 1810 John Spencer commenced manufacturing files which he took to Newcastle in creels on a donkey's back, and later added to his business the making of small castings and forgings. By 1830 steel converting and crucible shops had been added and the history of the steel works of Newburn followed the development of the railways of England for which they supplied much of the material. In 1872, under John Watson Spencer, the third in succession of the family, the works were enlarged and modernised, and in 1888 the business was formed into a limited company. By the beginning of the century it employed some two thousand men and boys and its products were world famous and were sent to almost every part of the world. The boiler plates, ship plates and the castings and forgings for the famous liner *Mauretania* were manufactured here, in addition to materials in connection with important contracts for the War Office, British Admiralty, and foreign navies. In 1916 the shops produced a weekly output of 1,500 tons of steel.'

An illustration of Newburn Old Hall drawn by H.T. Robinson in 1884. The building dates from the sixteenth century and in later years became part of Spencer's Works. This print was included in a centenary booklet produced by the company in 1910, however, not long after the building was demolished; swept away in the name of progress.

Spencer's Steel Works Brass Band in 1904. The North East has a fine tradition of brass bands but most people associate them with the mining industry. However, music was very popular for the workers in other industries as well. This must have been a successful band as they proudly display a large trophy. Competitions were held locally and nationally with the biggest of them all held at Crystal Palace in London.

A view of Spencer's Works from the south of the Tyne before the First World War. The chimneys are belching out smoke. Local people would have endured industrial pollution for years. These works were demolished in the 1930s.

Above: Some of the staff from Spencer's around 1912. There were a number of men who worked at the firm for over 40 years. One foreman, John Brown, was at Spencer's for 43 years – starting when he was 10 years old.

Left: William Elder on a NSU motorcycle in 1908. William lived at 93 Westmacott Street, Newburn and worked in the laboratories at Spencer's Steel Works.

John Spencer's Steel Works struggled in the Great Depression of the 1920s and went into liquidation. *Right*: An advert for the sale of property once owned by Spencer's. A newspaper at the time reported:

'Over 240 freehold houses and shops at Newburn, the property of John Spencer and Sons Ltd (now in liquidation) were included in the lots offered for sale ... at the County Hotel, Newcastle. There was a large attendance and the sum of £33,785 was realized as the result of the sale.'

Included in the sale were:

Nos 11 to 17, High Street. Block of stone-built cottages. Sold at £275.

Nos 6 to 21, Westmacott Street. Ten self-contained houses. Sold at £1,075.

No 2, Newburn Lane. Semi-detached residence. Sold at £400.

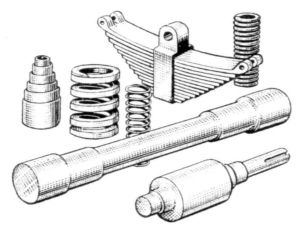

Above: Spencer's workers from 1946. Included are: Mr Reed, Ken Wright, Mrs Cuthbertson, Celia Shepherd, Joyce Mathison and Jackie Kelly.

Left: An advert for Spencer's from the 1950s. After liquidation a new company was formed in 1928 to manufacture parts for the railways and shipbuilding industry. This firm survived until the 1960s. Today, some of the former works buildings are still standing and in use.

The Glass Works

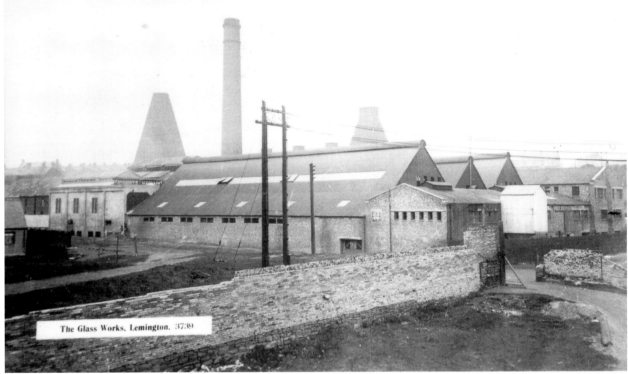

The Glass Works, Lemington. 3739

A postcard of Lemington Glass Works from the 1920s. Glass making started in Lemington in the 1780s and continued for over two hundred years. One of the cones of the Glass Works still stands today and is a prominent local landmark.

Lemington Glass Works Prize Band outside of Lemington House West in 1930. Back row: 2nd left Bill Barrass, 4th left George Ritson, 4th right James Crook, 3rd right Jack Cooper, 2nd right John Barrass, 1st right Mr Ferry. Second row: 1st left Mr Roscoe. Front row: 4th left Mr Foster, 2nd right Bob Taylor, 1st right Jack Taylor. The Band Master, in the front row centre, is Mr Miller.

The workforce of Lemington Glass Works in 1915. Only the names of two men are known – Johnny Curry and Charlie Danskin. However, included in the photograph are several members of the Barrass family – a well known name in the Glass Works.

The Glass Works' steam engine loaded with packing crates in the 1920s. This photograph was taken at Lemington Railway Station and the steam engine was used to transport goods from the works to the station.

Along The River

Newburn Bridge in the early 1900s – a vital link with the south of the Tyne. The bridge was built of iron in 1894 and there was a small toll to be paid to cross the River Tyne.

Newburn Bridge in 2011. It is still a popular crossing point for cars. There is no charge to cross but a set of traffic lights is needed to regulate the cars on the single lane bridge. This area is also popular for other traffic such as cyclists, walkers and, on the river, rowers. The Parish Church can be clearly seen on the 1900s photograph but today the view is blocked by trees.

A postcard sent from Newburn to Middlesbrough in 1915. The Steel Works are in the background and Newburn Bridge to the far right. On the left is Grange Road. Before the First World War there were the following businesses on the road: boot maker; hardware dealer; chemist; tobacconist and hairdresser; draper; newsagent; and the Newburn Branch of the Blaydon District Industrial Provident Society Limited (Co-op Store).

Lily Place on Newburn Bridge in 1903. She has milk pails with her. Lily is also seen on page 70 outside Joyce's Butchers. At the far end of the bridge, on the right, is the toll house. At this time the toll collector was Charles Henry Allcock. Tolls were collected from those crossing the bridge until 1947 when they finally ceased. It was the last bridge on the Tyne to charge a toll. To mark the occasion Councillors from Northumberland and Durham walked across the bridge for 'free'. At this time the River Tyne was the boundary between the old counties of Northumberland and Durham.

The riverside at Newburn around 1899. The Parish Church, Institute, Newburn Hotel and Boathouse Inn can all be seen. Newburn was expanding rapidly at this time and the population had doubled in the last ten years of the nineteenth century. Kelly's Directory has this description of the area in the early 1900s: 'The soil near the banks of the Tyne is of excellent quality; subsoil clay. The chief crops are wheat, oats, barley and turnips. The area of the township is 601 acres of land, 4 of water and 57 of tidal water; rateable value £17,948; the population in 1891 was 1,691, and of the parish, 5,624; the area of the urban district is 4,677 acres; rateable value £58,316; the population in 1897 was 7,963.'

The riverside in 2011. Many of the buildings by the riverbank in the photograph above have gone, including the railway signal box. However, still standing over a century later is the Boathouse Inn. On the wall of the pub are recorded the heights to which the river rose in the floods of 1771, 1815, 1850 and 1852. On the left is the Tyne Rowing Club – one of their crews can be seen on the river. The club had boathouses at Low Elswick and Scotswood before moving to Newburn in 1957. The Newburn boathouse was extended in 1999 with support from the University of Northumbria.

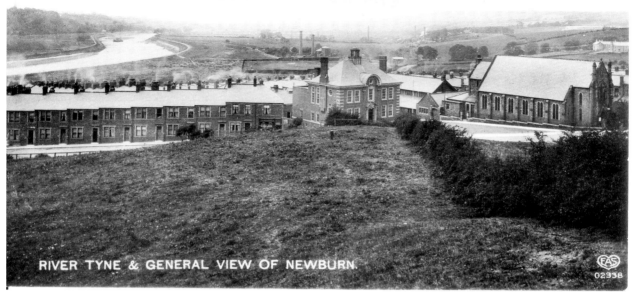

The River Tyne and general view of Newburn around 1912. In the centre are the Council Offices. To the left is the area now known as the Riverside Park. Behind the Council Offices, to the left, is the Water Pumping Station – now the Big Lamp Brewery and Keelman Pub. To the right is the Wesleyan Chapel.

A view of Newburn from the south side of the River Tyne in 1972.

A view of Newburn from the south side of the River Tyne in 2011.

Railways

The Station, Newburn.

Newburn Railway Station in the early 1900s. This photograph was taken from the level crossing leading to the Bridge. In the background, to the right, is the Newburn Hotel.

The site of the old Railway Station in 2011. There is nothing left of the old station or railway. Behind the trees to the right is the Newburn Hotel.

Newburn Railway Station – a photograph taken from the bridge over the lines. The station, opened in 1885, was on the Scotswood, Newburn & Wylam branch of the North Eastern Railway. The station master in the early 1900s was Robert Arthur. In the distance, to the left, are the chimneys of Spencer's Steel Works.

Lemington Railway Station around 1921. Robert Days is waiting on the platform fourth from the right wearing his Merchant Navy uniform. He was a wireless operator. Next to him is his friend Billy Kirton who has his uniform in the parcel on the platform. They are both off to sea.

Churches and Chapels

A postcard of the Wesleyan Chapel, Newburn.

In 2011 the Church has gone and in its place stands Chapel Court.

Above: Lemington United Methodist Church Union Choir outside the vestry facing Union Hall Road, around 1930. Back row: Mary Elliott, Margaret Carr, Jack Littleton, Mr Kennedy, Mr Halkier Jr, unknown, Mr Browell, Mrs Lowden. Third row: Mr Halkier (Choirmaster), Mrs Foster, Mrs Gill, Mrs Morgan, Mrs Pearson, Mrs Evans (Monty Pit Disaster widow), Mrs Fullerton, Mrs Kennedy. Second row: Phyllis Kennedy, Mrs Rendell, Mrs Browell, Mrs Urwin. Front row: Miss Duckham, Elsie Kennedy, Miss Duckham, Miss Palfrenan, Daisy Purvis, Marion Elliott.

The ladies at the front are displaying some of the fashions of the day with their short 'flapper' hairstyles and headbands. The older members of the Choir are much more formal and some of them are in their widow's black mourning clothes.

Mrs Evan's husband had lost his life at the Montegu Pit. The disaster occurred in 1925 when thirty-eight men were killed. Huge crowds attended the funerals of the pitmen.

Right: Lemington Primitive Methodist Church, on the corner of Loraine Terrace and Algernon Road, before the First World War. This church replaced an older Primitive Methodist Chapel in Low Lemington that had been built in 1863 at a cost of £300.

Right: Lemington Methodist Church in 2011. It was built in the 1890s and its predecessor in Low Lemington became an Infants School. A number of churches and chapels have disappeared from Lemington and Newburn but this place of worship is still open today. Little has changed from the photo above, although there is a later door on the side of the building.

Low Lemington Mission that was founded in 1904 by Thomas Gillan (*right*). Mr Gillan was noted for his open-air services using a wagon as a platform for his preaching. He also organised boat trips for members of the church.

Left: St Michael and All Angels Church, Newburn from a coloured postcard sent in 1938. The church was built in the 11th century, after a wooden building had burnt down, and it is believed that stone from the nearby Hadrian's Wall was used in its construction.

St. Michael and All Angels.   Newburn on Tyne.

Left: St Michael and All Angels Church in 2011, from a similar view as above. In the 19th century major renovation work took place that included seating for 400 people and a new organ. The clock was installed in the tower in 1865 to commemorate the Silver Jubilee of Queen Victoria.

Above: A postcard of the Vicarage, Newburn sent in 1912. The Reverend William Edward Nowell of University College, Durham was living in the Vicarage in the early 1900s

Left: The interior of St Michael and All Angels Church around 1913.

Right: A postcard of the Holy Saviour's Church, Sugley, Lemington-on-Tyne. It was sent from Lemington to Medomsley in County Durham in 1904. The message on the back reads: 'This is a view of the Parish Church close to where I am living.' Some people are relaxing in the grounds of the church and pose for the photographer.

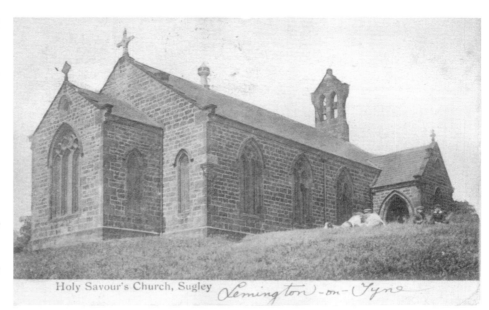

Holy Savour's Church, Sugley *Lemington-on-Tyne*

Right: The Holy Saviour's Church in 2011. The church was built in 1837 and was consecrated by the Bishop of Durham, the Right Reverend Edward Maltby. The following year a school was opened. The school survived until 1936 and schoolmasters included: Mr Wood, Mr Sladin, Mr Price, Mr Clark and Mr Browell.

Right: Four local clergymen in 1883. They are Canon John Reed (sitting on the right) with Reverends C.A. Fox, W.I. Ground and William O'Brady Jones.

Canon Reed died the following year at the age of eighty-one. In 1832 Cholera struck the area. At that time John Reed was the curate of Ryton and he took charge of the parish of Newburn after the Vicar, Reverend J. Edmonson died of the disease. No one was allowed to enter or leave the area and black flags warned people to stay away. Food was left for those well enough to collect it. Reverend Reed bravely led the church services and read over the burials until the quarantine was over.

In June 1919 Reverend Fox died at the age of seventy-six. For forty-eight years he had served as curate of Newburn and vicar of Sugley.

Younger Days

No 26 Lemington 'Newburn Hall' Scouts Camp at Rothbury in the early 1950s. Mr Tasker and Mr Humble are with the scouts.

Newburn & District Schoolboys, 1951. Back row: Mr Laidler (Secretary), W. Dance, W. Wheeler, N. Campbell, L. Dodds, Mr Norton (Chairman), E. Ormston, L. Clarke, Mr McAndrew (Treasurer). Middle row: D. Dockerty, R. Norman, T. Brown, C. Westwood. Front row: T. Robson, E. Stewart, W. Creighton and J. Hetherington.

Above: Newburn Hall School class in 1953. Back row: Billy Thompson, Raymond Dick, George Clark, Mary Dawn, Janet Hall, J. McDooley. Third row: Robert Jackson, Derek Taylor, Brian Jackson, Richard Proud, Robert Emmerson, Eric Beofield. Second row: Mary Dawson, Irene Kappeno, Margaret Scondle, Norma Fisher, Jean Thompson, Doreen Scott, Jean Hartley, unknown. Front row: Derek Ideson, John Mills, Jimmy Frame and Eddie Purry.

Right: Outside Lemington Secondary School in June 1939 are, from right, Doris Coulson, Rita Boyd and Jean Tate. A few months after this photograph was taken the lives of these three girls would be very different. The start of the Second World War in September 1939 would give them gas masks, the black out, bombing and rationing.

A group from Sugley Church School in the 1920s. Back row: Mr Clark (Headmaster), Florrie Forrester, Isabelle Isbone, Harriet Haw, Mary Watson, Madge Clarkson, Jennie Isbone. Third row: Lily Watson, Nellie Cheek, Violet Curry, Bella Maughan, Elsie Clarkson, Jennie Robson, ? Forrester. Second row includes: Stanley Robson, Elsie Cheek, Leslie Cheek and ? Currie. Front row includes: Ronnie Maughan, Tot Robson, Ernest Cheek and Longstaff.

Sugley Church School group around 1931. Back row includes: Miss McKay (far left), Foster, Falkus, Bobby Henderson, Henry Smith and Mrs Brown on the right. Front row includes: John Dolan, Falkus, John Hetherington and Arthur Smith.

Newburn Manor School football team around 1936. Back row: Mr Beal (Headmaster), R. Johnson, W. Braithwaite, unknown, Mansfield, Caruthers, Humble. Middle row: Lowrie, J. Veitch, J. Ormston, S. Urwin, N. Callender, L. Walker. Front row: R. Temperley, F. Lambert and Walker.

Newburn Manor School netball team in 1943. Back row: Jean Patterson, Miss McNab, Thelma Straughn, Elsie Mansfield. Front row: Isabelle Edgar, Betty Coe, Rose Johnson, and Joyce Campbell.

Bell's Close

St George's RC School and Church, Bell's Close around 1908 with some of the pupils standing outside. Only one child's name is known – in the front row, ninth from the right is Thomas Grady. The church was built in 1869 and the school six years later. In 1898 the school was enlarged to accommodate 566 children, although when this photograph was taken the average was 340.

Bell's Close Catholic Men's Club outing around 1947. Back row: ? Percy, unknown, J. Spillett, Robert O'Neill, C. Brown, ? Riley, unknown, ? Gair, unknown, H. Dolan, J. Peace, W. O'Hara, M. Thompson, unknown. Third row: unknown, unknown, unknown, unknown, ? Bamburgh, Bobby Logue, unknown, J. McSwaine, unknown, unknown, Thomas Grady, Hugh Logan, Anthony Lenaghan. Second row: ? Corrigan, ? O'Boyle, unknown, unknown, Father Cassidy, Joseph Loughran, unknown, unknown, ? Riley, ? Logan, unknown, unknown, D. Garland. First row: J. Hodgson, unknown, J. Gair, W. Usher, Jimmy Grady, J. Fay, John Fay, unknown, unknown, ? Failey, ? Roseby, unknown and Patrick Grady.

Bell's Close Wesleyans AFC. They played in the Newcastle District United Churches League. Football was so popular at that this time that there were numerous leagues – including ones for schools, churches and apprentices. This photograph shows them when they were League winners in 1924-25. In the back row, third from left is Fred Moore. Fourth from the left is George Moore (goalkeeper). Both were shipyard workers. This photograph is believed to be taken shortly before the Montegu (Monty) Pit Disaster when a number of members of the club lost their lives.

Bell's Close Welfare football team, 1933-34. Jim Barclay is on the grass on the left. George Barclay is in the back row, second player from the right. George Surtees, who was weighman at the Monty Pit, is seated on the right.

Working Lives

People getting on and off a Newcastle Corporation Tramways car No 283 in Lemington in 1946. The tram was on its way to Throckley.

Newcastle Corporation Tram No 308 at Lemington in 1935. The remains of the old Iron Works are to the left. To the right is the painting firm of J. Liddell & Son. The tram is on the loop that allowed vehicles to pass each other.

A postcard of the Newburn Hotel and Grange Road. The photographer was standing on the bridge at Newburn Railway Station. In the early 1900s the landlord of the Newburn Hotel was George Milburn.

The Newburn Hotel in 2011. Sadly, this pub, like many these days, is closed and awaiting a new landlord.

The Boathouse Inn public house, around 1900. The landlord at this time was John Hall. The pub and the houses to the right are in Water Row with the railway signal box on the far right.

The Boathouse in 2011 is still a popular pub for a drink by the river. The signal box, like all evidence of the railway in Newburn, has been removed.

The Water Pumping Station, Newburn in 1996. It was built in the 1850s for Whittle Dene Water Company to extract river water and was derelict for many years. The site was rebuilt as pub, brewery and bed & breakfast in 1997. This is also a Jimmy Forsyth photograph.

The Big Lamp Brewery and the Keelman pub in 2011. Also on this site is the Keelman's Lodge Bed & Breakfast. The Brewery originally started in the Big Lamp area of Newcastle in 1982 and now supplies traditionally brewed fine ales to pubs throughout the country.

Shopping

In the days before supermarkets, most people shopped in their local area and perhaps only travelled to Newcastle for special purchases. Most needs were catered for locally and here are a few images of shops and services in Lemington and Newburn.

Inside the Blaydon Co-op Pharmacy in the 1950s. The pharmacy was on Tyne View and is pictured on the middle photograph on the facing page. An advert for the Blaydon Co-op from the 1930s said: 'The Stores can supply your every need. Everything that you require – everything that you desire. Food, furnishings, draperies, boots and shoes in endless variety. Will you call at Lemington or any of our branches.'

LEMINGTON
Shoe Repair Service

Practical Boot & Shoe Repairers.

Best English Leather.
First Class Workmanship.
Up-to-date Machinery.
Orders Collected and
Delivered.

Give us a Trial—
Satisfaction Guaranteed
Tyne View, Lemington

All Judges of Butter
who once purchase our
FAMOUS DANISH
pronounce it to be

THE BUTTER : PAR EXCELLENCE

and become Regular Customers
at

The May-Dew Dairy

THE BUTTER SHOP,
LEMINGTON

Above: An advert from the 1930s for the May-Dew Dairy, Lemington with 'Butter: Par Excellence'.

Left: An advert for Lemington Shoe Repair Service, Tyne View, from the 1930s. They offered: 'First Class Workmanship – Up-to-date Machinery.'

Here are three photographs showing how Tyne View has changed over the past 100 years.

Top right: A postcard sent in 1904 that shows George Robson, grocer, in the centre. Also on Tyne View at this time was Matthew Garland, hairdresser; Andrew Nasbitt, teacher of music; Arthur Thompson, boot and shoe maker; and Mrs Priscilla Short, Post Office.

Middle right: A similar view of Tyne View from the 1950s. Blaydon Co-op Pharmacy is on the left. On the far right is the main Co-op Store that was demolished in the 1990s.

Bottom right: A view of Tyne View in 2011. The Co-op Pharmacy has now been replaced by Boots and the site of the Co-op Store is now The Lemington Centre. This photograph was taken on a quiet Sunday morning when no shoppers were around!

Left: G. Hugel Pork Butcher, Station Road, Newburn, around 1912. A few years later this German-owned shop was closed when the First World War started. On the window is written: 'Noted for Sausages & Hams, Pies Etc'. Hanging in the window are dozens of sausages with what looks like pies and black puddings below them. The shop later became Bolam's Greengrocers.

Right: R.W Joyce's Butchers, No 33 Boyd Street, Newburn in 1928. Outside the shop are Norman Joyce and his sister-in-law Lily Joyce (née Place).

Below: An advert for M.J. Gill, Rokerby Street, Lemington, 1930s. 'Noted for Home-Cooked Ham and Tongue'.

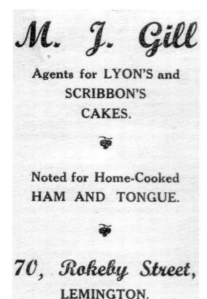

Above: Bolam's Greengrocers, Station Road, Newburn in 1936. There is an excellent display of fruit and vegetables in the window

Days to Remember

Lemington Tennis Club, Montague Street, around 1920. Back row: unknown, Mr Dowie, George Coates, Leslie Harris, Leslie Philipson, unknown, unknown, unknown, Tom Dowie, unknown, Frank Gray. Middle row: unknown, ? Darwin, Mollie Gibson, Aaron Rencastle, unknown, unknown, Mary Leyborne, Alice Coates. Front row: unknown, Harry Rencastle, Ella Grey, Nellie Graham, Billy Clark, Winnie Gray, unknown, Alice Graham. Tennis was much more formal in those days – no shorts or mini skirts! The men wore crisp white shirts and trousers while the ladies wore long skirts and blouses. On the grass in front of them are their wooden rackets that are very different from today's hi-tech, carbon fibre equipment.

Right: Newburn Fire Station Brigade around 1910. The service was originally run by Spencer's Steel Works before it was later taken over by the local authority. On each fireman's jacket is a badge with a number. Number '1' is Mr Murray, while '2' is Mr Blakey and '8' Mr Wardlaw. Were numbers a way of identifying each man? Hanging from their belts are an axe and a roll of string.

A Peace Day street party looking from Low to High Lemington in 1919. Unlike the Second World War, when street parties were held immediately after Victory in Europe and then Victory in Japan, events such as this Peace Tea were held around the country a year after the end of the First World War. Most Peace Day parties were centred around events for children with games, sports, processions and dressing up. On this photograph, at the back of the group, is a decorated cart with smartly dressed children on board. On the cart are members of the Wilkinson family who were haulage contractors. At the front right are members of a schoolboy football team and behind them are young people dressed as nurses, sailors and soldiers. Some of them are holding a banner proclaiming 'Victory' and 'Peace'. How many in this photograph lost loved ones in what was called 'The Great War' or the 'War to End All Wars'?

Newburn Manor School around 1925. Back row: unknown, Muriel Johnson, Tinnion, unknown, unknown, Milburn Grayson, Mrs Palmer (husband killed in First World War). Third row unknown, unknown, Mary Hutchinson, Florrie Swinbank, Martha Winter, unknown, unknown.

Second row: Ena Nelson, Nora Callendar, unknown, Sally Walker, Jean White, unknown. Front row: Brayson, Tommy Jordan (later a scout for Newcastle United and also ran Newburn AFC), Telford, Howard Jopson, unknown, unknown.

A procession of the Comrades of the Great War, Newburn around 1920. They are passing what is now the traffic lights by the bank and post office. The band is followed by men who either served or had friends and family who served in the First World War. To the right, several young boys have joined the procession – how many of them would be involved in the Second World War twenty years later? The horrors of the Great War left a lasting impression on communities who lost sons, brothers and husbands in the conflict. Newburn, like many districts, erected a War Memorial with the names of those who had been killed.

Newburn & District War Memorial in 2011. Ninety years previously this area was packed with dignitaries, servicemen, a military band and local people when the Memorial was unveiled.

If today you say 'The Hoppings' most people will think of the annual fair on Newcastle's Town Moor, however the word 'Hoppings' originally referred to any local fair. Here we have the Hoppings at Newburn with Hoadley's Shooting Gallery in 1900. The site is believed to be the High Street with Newburn House (belonging to Dr Scott) in the background.

People made their own entertainment in the 1920s and here is the Lemington Gala of 1927. Events such as these were very popular and gave people the chance to dress up – the ever popular cowboy and indian costumes at the front.

Above: The Prince of Wales Theatre, Lemington, around 1925. This picture palace was built in 1924 by John Grantham who became Lord Mayor of Newcastle in 1936. Today we watch the movies in multiplexes in Newcastle or the Metro Centre, however, for many years most communities had their own cinema.

Right: An advert for the Prince of Wales Theatre from the 1930s. It says the theatre is: 'A home from home … where everybody goes.'

For the Super Shows

PAY A VISIT TO THE

Prince of Wales Theatre,
Lemington,

Continuous except Saturday.
Sunday at 8 p.m.

A Home from Home
Where everybody goes

Left: The original Tyne Iron public house in 1939. It was nicknamed 'The Hairy Man'. Other pubs in Lemington in the early part of the 20th century were The Donnelly, Dr Syntax and the Glasshouse Inn. At Bell's Close was the Lamb and Flag.

The official opening of Newburn Council Offices in 1911. Councillors in the early 1900s included: Richard Armstrong, Amos Benn, Isaac Taylor Chessman, William Davidson, John Eggie, Matthew Kirton, Charles Nicholson, Edward Nicholson, Henry Nicholson, Edward Stanley and James Stewart.

Lemington Male Voice Choir and the Northumbria Police Band at a concert in 1975.

Newburn Rose Park in 1956. It was officially opened by former Newburn Councillor, Mr George M. Brown MP. This land belonged to the Duke of Northumberland who allowed its use by Newburn Council for a 'peppercorn rent' of one rose a year. In 1973 the 10th Duke of Northumberland unveiled a memorial to his brother, the 9th Duke, who was killed during the Second World War while serving with the Grenadier Guards.

The Park and War Memorial in 2011.

A 'Best Wishes from Newburn' postcard. The views are, top row, left to right: Schools; Institute; and Village. Middle row: Station; and Parish Church. Bottom row: Warkworth Crescent; and Station Road. On the right is a picture of the Lych Gate, Newburn Church.

A group of people outside the Picturedrome and Variety Palace, Westmacott Street, Newburn in 1912. The poster in the centre is advertising a 'Grand Variety Programme' that night. This photograph is something of a mystery. Why are nearly everyone holding up one finger? Perhaps a reader may know why.

Acknowledgements

The authors would like to thank the following who have helped with the publication of this book:

Members of the West Newcastle
Picture History Collection:

Harry Bennett, Cliff Kirkham, Fred Millican,
Bill Stuart, Linda Sutton and Mike Young.

Sharyn Taylor for typing the manuscript.

The staff of the West End Customer Service Centre
and Library, Newcastle.

Bibliography

Bygone Bell's Close & Lemington

Centenary of John Spencer & Sons

Kelly's Directory of
Durham & Northumberland, 1902

Newburn in Old Picture Postcards

Newburn Official Guide, 1937

Newburn Official Guide, 1958

Newburn Urban District Official Guide, 1972

'Our Parish' – Parish Church of the
Holy Saviour, Sugley

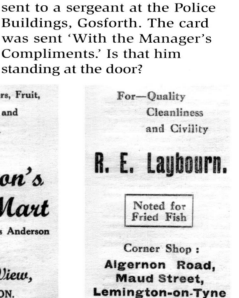

A trade card from the North Eastern Bank, Newburn. It was sent to a sergeant at the Police Buildings, Gosforth. The card was sent 'With the Manager's Compliments.' Is that him standing at the door?

Here are some adverts from the 1930s that show the variety of shops in the area before the Second World War.

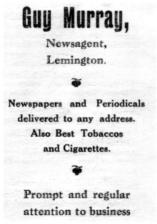

Guy Murray,

Newsagent,
Lemington.

Newspapers and Periodicals
delivered to any address.
Also Best Tobaccos
and Cigarettes.

Prompt and regular
attention to business

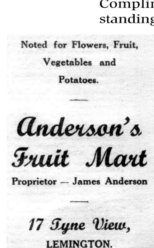

Noted for Flowers, Fruit,
Vegetables and
Potatoes.

*Anderson's
Fruit Mart*

Proprietor — James Anderson

17 Tyne View,
LEMINGTON.

For—Quality
Cleanliness
and Civility

R. E. Laybourn.

Noted for
Fried Fish

Corner Shop :
**Algernon Road,
Maud Street,
Lemington-on-Tyne**

J. W. Johnson, M.P.S.

Dispensing Chemist,

3 TYNE VIEW, LEMINGTON.

Glendinning's Beevinalt, Hall's Wine, Vibrona, Wincarnis,
Invalid Port, Burgundy, and other Wines always in stock

Sick Room Requisites   Toilet Articles of all kinds
National Health Insurance Dispensing

Photography :—
Kodak Films, Papers, Developers etc.
First-Class Developing & Printing Service

Wm. Irwin Thompson,

OF ROKEBY STREET
IS NOTED FOR
**Finest Bacon and Ham
Home-Cooked Ham
Danish Butter**

Try our Specially Blended Tea

Our Speciality : Freshly Ground Coffee
Note the address—Foot of Rokeby Street.

West Newcastle Picture History Collection

West Newcastle Picture History Collection was created in 1984 to collect and maintain an archive of images illustrating the history and heritage of West Newcastle. The collection now contains over 14,000 photographs and documents that illustrate and record streets, pubs, shops, schools, churches, events and places of work from the 19th century to the present. The bulk of the images relate to Scotswood, Benwell, Elswick, Fenham and Arthur's Hill but also includes items relating to Denton, Lemington, Newburn, Throckley and Westerhope.

The collection continues to grow through donations and other sources of photographs old and new. Copies of images from the collection can be purchased as photocopies or as laser prints from computer files.

The collection is open to visitors on Monday mornings between 9.30 am and 12 pm; Monday afternoons between 2 pm and 4 pm; and Thursday afternoons between 2 pm and 4 pm and at other times by arrangement with library staff.

The original home of the collection was Benwell Library but in 2008 moved to the West End Customer Service Centre and Library on Condercum Road, Newcastle.

One of the 14,000 photographs in the West Newcastle Picture History Collection – Newburn High Street, around 1900.

Also available from Summerhill Books

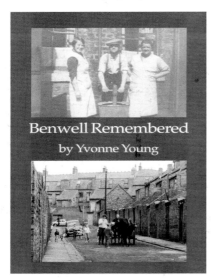

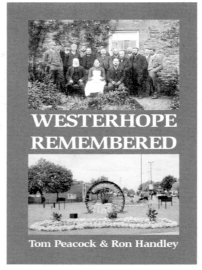

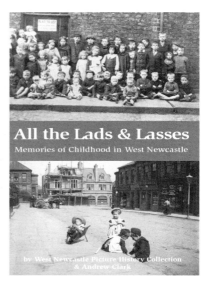

Benwell Remembered
Yvonne Young remembers life in this Newcastle community. With memories of local people and over 160 photographs.

Westerhope Remembered
Historians, Tom Peacock & Ron Handley, tell the story of Westerhope with memories of residents and 130 photographs.

All The Lads & Lasses
Memories of Childhood in West Newcastle – over 120 old photographs recall schooldays, entertainment and family life.

www.summerhillbooks.co.uk